GOD Is Real and So Are HIS Promise

Have you ever wondered if GOD and HIS promises are real? I'll list three right now, but at the end of my book I'll list all my favorites. I'm not trying to force anyone to believe in GOD, that's between you and your belief. I just want to share somethings that I know that I know that I know, had to be GOD that got me thru it. Some of these things are so phenomenal. Maybe you should look up the meaning of that word, because you may think some of these didn't happen. But with GOD as my witness, it did. After I tell you most of the things I've been thru, I'm going to cover subjects like,

1) Is GOD - JESUS real?

2) Faith and does GOD hear our prayers?

3) Does GOD give us dreams?

4)Are angels and spirits real?

5) Is prophecy real?

6) Can we really speak things into existence?

7)Bullies. There are no scriptures about it, but we know there are stories with bullies in them.

8) What the bible says about?

Here are the three scriptures I said I would share.

Matthew 7th chapter 7th and 8th verse.

7. ASK, AND IT SHALL BE GIVEN YOU; SEEK AND YOU SHALL FIND;

KNOCK, AND IT SHALL BE OPEN UNTO YOU.

8. FOR EVERYONE THAT ASKETH RECEIVETH; AND HE THAT SEEKETH FINDETH; AND TO HIM THAT KNOCKETH IT SHALL BE OPENED. I love this scripture because it's in all caps. In the bible, when scriptures are written in all caps or written in red ink, it means GOD is talking. I also love the word shall. When GOD says shall in scriptures, HE's not saying it may be, or it can be, HE's telling you it SHALL be.

Jeremiah 29th chapter and the 13th verse. AND YE SHALL SEEK ME, AND FIND ME, WHEN YE SHALL SEARCH FOR ME WITH ALL YOUR HEART. This one means all you had to do is be sincere in your prayers, know that HE's really listening to your every word. You had to have faith and no doubt that GOD is going to answer your prayers.

Jeremiah 32:27 BEHOLD, I AM THE LORD, THE GOD OF ALL FLESH: IS THERE ANYTHING TO HARD FOR ME?

Not a thing, you half to have faith. Joel Osteen told Steve Harvey this story about staying on faith street. I'm asking everyone to check it out. Just go to You Tube, click on search, type in Steve Harvey – Stay on Faith Street. It's very uplifting and may help you a whole lot.

Is GOD – JESUS Real?

Now I'm going to share some of the things that happened to me in my lifetime.

1) This is a true story, before seatbelts were enforced, I was downtown with my son Timothy who was just 2 at the time. He was standing in the front seat with his back leaning against the seat, we were sitting at a red light. When the light turned green, I took off. Right when I took off this KC power and light truck ran his red light. When we should have heard the sound of a terrible wreck, we didn't. Instead his truck went right thru my car without even touching it. In what seemed to be slow motion I turned and looked at him and he looked at me and both of us kept going. Years passed and I kept asking GOD about the incident. I was watching Touched by An Angel and this episode showed a bus full of kids and how this car did the exact same thing. It showed the car going thru the school bus in slow motion and both of those kept going. I had my answer then. To me that was GOD saying, I take care of those whom are mine.

2.) I was at a red light. I was driving a car called a pacer. It looks like a big ole round ladybug. I had the tail gate up and Timothy and Tiffany were riding back there. My light turned green and I was about to pull off when this old song came on the radio called Melinda. I stopped, turned it up, said Melinda and swayed from side to side. I got ready to pull off and this car came thru the red light doing at least 70. I slammed on the brakes. Had I not that car would have hit me, and Tiffany and Timothy would have flown out the back.

3.) This happened Thanksgiving night 2018. I was driving my son Terry's SUV and believe me, the 5 days I had it my son kept saying, don't wreck my truck.   I'd say, I'm not. I was taking my granddaughter Ne'Kole home and on the way back as I got real close to my home, I said, I told Terry I wasn't going to wreck his truck. I watched this utility truck headed my way cross the line and then go back to his side, he did that 3 times and the third time to my side he came. I started honking and honking but he stayed on my side. There was nowhere to pull over because there was nothing but ditches and if I would have went off I would have turned the SUV over. When I saw he wasn't going to go back on his side, I just turned the SUV off and closed my eyes and waited for the head on collision. At the last minute he turned and the whole side of his driver's side went along the whole side of my driver's side, front to back, but he kept going. No one got the license number and because it was Thanksgiving night, I couldn't get the police to come. I had to go to them. The truck was drivable, but the insurance company totaled the truck. I have been told by the doctor that I needed surgery on my back and there would be a 50/50 chance of me walking. For years I kept having this reoccurring dream that I was in a wheelchair, but each time I had it I would say, I rebuke that. And I still rebuke it.

4.) Back in 1977 Kansas City had the worst flood ever. The water completely covered this store that was on 350 Highway and Cleveland. They have raised the street since then so if we ever did have another flood it wouldn't affect that area. This is the truth, when the water finally went down, there were cars stacked on top of each other like someone had done that on purpose. Timothy was 2 years old then and we were down on Cleveland

and 18th at a car shop having some work done on the car. When we left it was barely raining so I decided to go over to my friend's house. We were on the porch talking and the rain started coming down hard. I told him I better leave so I could get home safely. By the time I got to Prospect the water looked like a small stream coming down that street, so I turned around and went back to my friend's house, but they had left. So off again I went. When I got to Prospect, I had to decide if I wanted to cross it because the water had picked up real bad coming down that street. Now this time the rain was coming down even harder. I decided to cross prospect and cars started coming down the street like boats in the water. I made it across safely and was saying in my mind how I was on 31st street and had to get to 47th street. I started out at 4:00 PM in the afternoon and I did not get to 47th St until it was starting to get dark outside. Just about every way I try to go was flooded. Then this firetruck pulled in behind me and was following me and honking. It seemed like everywhere I went it wanted to go. I couldn't get out of the way because there was no way to pull over, so I kept going until finally it left. The next time I saw the firetruck it was stuck in water. By this time, I was crying because I didn't see any way to get to my mom's house. Timothy touched my shoulder and said, it's ok mama, everything is going to be alright, then he started singing JESUS loves me. Keep in mind he was 2, how I even understood what he said was something. I kept going around till I saw a way that I could get to my mom's house. It was thru this vacant lot that no one had ever driven thru or wanted to walk thru, when it was dry, but I was going to try it no matter what. I sat there for a few minutes to look over the whole lot and then I took off. I was going so fast the car was zigzagging different ways and then I hit this bump and the car flew up in the air, I stayed up there for a few minutes and then hit the ground hard. The car swerved a little, finally I got it in control and went down the hill and turned the corner and there was my mom's house. When I stop the car in front of her house, I began to thank GOD and praise HIM like I've never done before. The next day when I talk to this guy that lived up by the lot. He didn't believe that I came thru there because he said, even when it's dry, people can't make it thru there. GOD got me thru, thank you GOD.

5.) I'm a true believer that GOD will have you in the right place at the right time. I had to go down to Swope Parkway Health Center to pick up my medicine so I asked my niece Treva if I could drive her car and she said she had something she had to do. Because my sister Margaret had dialysis the next day, I decided I'd wait until the day after to go down to Swope. When I did get to go down there, I walked through the door and there was this lady and her mother who was in a wheelchair. When I got to the point where they were the young lady said, GOD told me you would be here today and that you were supposed to pray for me, so I did, in the right place at the right time.

6.) Margaret, who is my oldest sister asked me if I would take her to her doctor's appointment. I told her I would. On the day of her appointment, Treva's car got a flat tire so Margaret ended up rescheduling her appointment. They rescheduled it for Tuesday and on that day, Margaret called me and asked if I had remembered I'd said I would take her to the doctor's office and I didn't, so I had to hurry and get dressed. But let me say this, the day before, I was in my prayer room and I was praying to GOD that HE would bless her with the home she needed so she could have a room where she could do her dialysis, but I also ask the LORD to give us a dialysis nurse that would come over and do her dialysis. She's always complaining about how cold it is where she has her dialysis so being in her own home would be the best thing ever. I was so glad that I had prayed that prayer because like I said, I always believe that GOD has you in the right place at the right time. Because I had transportation, I decided to call Swope Parkway Health Center to go and pick up some medicine that I wasn't able to get the last time I was up there, so I called them and I asked the lady if I could come and get it. She said no because my insurance wouldn't pay for it until tomorrow. I kind of laughed because I knew there must have been a good reason why I couldn't get it that day. I was right. When I got Margaret to her appointment, I decided I wasn't going to get out of the car, but I sat there for a few minutes and something kept saying go inside, so I got my stuff and went inside. As I was sitting there this young lady got off the elevator. She was talking to someone about still being a dialysis nurse, so when she passed, I stopped her and started talking to her. I asked her about her being a dialysis nurse and she said yes she was and I asked her if she was interested in coming to somebody's home and help them do there dialysis there. She started crying. She said yesterday I was just asking GOD to bless me with another job because she wasn't used to not having 2 jobs. Now keep in mind I had just ask GOD myself yesterday if HE would bless us with a home and a dialysis nurse. As she was talking the spirit told me that her daughter was very gifted, so I begin to tell her what the spirit told me. I said your daughter is very gifted and she started crying again. She told me how she had had stem cell surgery and her doctor had told her that she would never have any more kids after the surgery. After the surgery, a year or so more she found out she was pregnant. She had a daughter, and the little girl had a birthmark on her in the same place her scar was where she had her surgery. In every detail, the scar was identical to her birth mark. She told me she felt like that was GOD's way of telling her, I'm GOD, I can do anything I want. I have the last say in any and everything. And I knew why I had to be in the right place the whole time and not leave to go pick up my medicine that day.

7.) I'm always asking GOD to send me something or show me a sign. Some people get birds, some get butterflies, our family gets both. I remembered how Linda, who is my youngest sister, told me that she looks out the window and sees a red bird every time she wants to hear from GOD. So, I decided I'd ask GOD for one. I prayed to GOD and I asked HIM for a red bird, the next day right outside my window on a bush, there was a red bird. Just so people can see, I took a picture of it. But you know how some people are, we always want more, so the next day I asked GOD again if HE would send me a red bird. Before the week was out, here comes my red bird. I asked GOD can I see a red bird again, next day there was red bird right there on the bush. I decided I'd do something different. I asked GOD to send me a blue jay. Before the week was out, there was one on the bush. I took a picture of it also. But then, I remembered seeing this bird on TV on a commercial that I had never seen before. It was a brown bird with little yellow spots on his belly, so I asked God to send me that bird. Before the week was out, I heard this noise on the window, so I went to look and there was the bird that I had asked for and he looked like he was trying to get into the house. I took a picture of it and then I went close to the window and he flew away. I took it kind of comical and said that was GOD's way of saying, OK, alright already, I sent you every bird you asked for!

8.) I have moved since I had asked GOD for those birds. Years have gone by, but where I lived I have a back porch. I decided I'd ask GOD to allow a bird to land on the back porch. I said LORD, I haven't seen a red or blue bird in years, so I'm asking YOU to send me a red one. A couple of days went by, no bird, so under my breath I said LORD, I asked YOU to send me a bird, but even before I could get the word bird out of my mouth this blue Jay came squawking real loud past my window. I decided I'd follow the sound because it sounded like it had landed on my back porch, so I went to check and even though I saw the bird, it wasn't on my back porch but it was there, and it was a blue Jay so I decided I'd call my twin sister Annette and tell her about how that bird came by my window so loud where I could hear and she said funny you should say something about that, I was in my kitchen standing by the back door drinking a cup of hot chocolate and this red bird landed on my back porch. She said the moment I saw it I said, Jeanette here's your red bird. I don't even remember telling her that I had asked GOD about sending me the bird, but she is my twin, Twin connection maybe.

9.) I was over to my parent's house, and my dad asked me to change the lock on the back door. It was almost getting dark outside and I was struggling to get this lock off the door. After getting frustrated, I decided I'd stop and pray. I asked GOD to give me the knowledge to get the lock off the door. Even before I got an answer, I started trying to take the lock off, still it wouldn't come off. After about a half hour or so went by, I stopped, and started talking to GOD again. In an upset tone, I said LORD, I asked if YOU would help me get this lock off. Immediately, GOD said to me, you asked ME, but you didn't wait to hear what I had to say. Instead, you just went right back into trying to take that lock off the door. This is what you need to do. HE told me exactly how to get that lock off, I did what HE said, and pop to the floor went the lock. All I had to do was wait and listen.

 10.)One night I was watching Americas next top model on tv and I decided that at 2:00 AM, I was going to pray, because usually when I pray to GOD at 2:00 o'clock in the morning, HE usually moves the next day, 2 days later, or even a week or month or so, but it doesn't take long before HE answers. I started to watch Americas next top model and when 2:00 o'clock came, I looked up at the clock and I decided I wanted to see who won before I went to do the prayer and the TV froze. I couldn't watch anything, so immediately I started praying.

11.) There was this lady I knew, and the spirit told me to tell her not to drive her car, so I did. She took her car to have it serviced and the man told her it was a good thing she wasn't driving it other than to come have it serviced because her car was like a time bomb ready to explode.

12.) One night I was crying and praying to the LORD and asking HIM to bless me with a good job. The next day Linda came over and asked if I wanted to go out to Bendix- Allied Signal to put in for a job. We went, put in for the job. Later that day I was at the laundromat washing and she came rushing in and said I had gotten the job, but they didn't.

13.) In November of 91 Bendix-Allied Signal decided to lay off some people, and I was one of them. Before they laid me off, they laid off a group of over 500 people. When it came time for me to be laid off, they decided to lay off 499 people. All they had to do was lay off 1 more person and they wouldn't had had to pay our group $429.00 a week for 6 months. The group before us got no pay. But GOD would not allow them to lay off one more person, so not only did we get the money, we also got free groceries each month as well. GOD is so awesome!

14.) My daughter Tammy came to me one day and told me she was going to go get a car. She was 19 at the time and I remember thinking she was going to have to have a cosigner or something, but she wasn't going to be able to just get a car. She left with a friend and next thing I know she's driving into the driveway with a new car. That's how GOD moves. HE has the final say so on everything.

15.) I had a cousin named Floyd. He has passed away now but he had seizures. He stayed on the 3rd floor of the home that I used to stay in. We used to worry about him being up there all by himself, so I took a bat up there to him and told him, whenever he felt like he was going to have a seizure to bang the back on the floor and we'd come up there. I heard the bat banging on the floor, so I went running up there and he was having a seizure. We helped him out of the seizure, and I thanked him for banging the bat on the floor. He said he had taken the bat downstairs and forgot to bring it back upstairs. So, who banged a bat on the floor? Thank YOU for that one GOD.

16.) I like to play Nintendo games and I have a lot of them. This friend called me and told me she and some kids were coming over. Because I knew that one of them like to steal, I hid some of my important games. When she came over it was just her and her son. We talked for a while and got a lot of things done. She left so I went back to play my game and I realized they were gone, but I had forgotten I had hidden them. I accused her son of taking them. I tried to call her, but she didn't answer so I tried most of the night to call her. After a while I jumped into the church van and tried to go over to her house, but the van wouldn't start. I went back into the house and tried calling her again. The next day I tried calling her again and she didn't answer. Then I remembered I had hidden the games and went and got them. I needed to figure out why the van wouldn't start, so I went out to try to start it and I realized that it was in neutral and that's why I couldn't start it. When I put it in park, it started right up. I thanked GOD because I realized that had I had accused that boy of stealing something he didn't, I could have scarred him for life. Thank YOU, GOD for not letting that van start or her answering the phone.

17.) When I was going to DeVry college, I had to ride the bus there and back home. It was very cold this day and there was snow on the ground, so I decided I'd catch an early bus to get to school and if I had to catch 2 different buses then I just had to catch 2 different buses. It was just too cold to be standing there. When a bus came, I got on it. I decided I'd get off on 75th St and wait for my bus. When I got off on 75th St there was this little old white lady trying to get her car going that was stuck in the snow by the curb. I probably had a while to wait for my bus, so I walked over and asked her if she needed help, but I noticed to the side of me there were these 2 white guys sitting and watching her from their car. I braced my foot up against the curb and told her to try to go, she couldn't move but she tried again and this time her car pulled free. But at that same moment these 2 guys decide to get out of the car and asked if I needed help. I told them no, I didn't need any help. She offered to pay but I didn't take the money. I walked back to my bus stop and just when I got up to the stop, my bus that I needed to get on came. I got on the bus and was sitting there reading my Bible and the spirit begin to talk to me and said, the reason why I ended up getting on the 1st bus and helping this little old lady was because those 2 white men were planning to rob her and that's why HE sent me to help her get out of the snow. GOD is so good.

I wanted you all to read those stories because I wanted you to see that GOD - JESUS is real, how HE moves, and how HE always haves you in the right place at the right time. You have a lot of people in this world that believe more in the devil then they do GOD or JESUS. It's so sad to me because all they half to do is look around. You can see GOD in the trees, the flowers, the birds, the grass, the stars, the moon and the sun, even in inventions that people make. I feel like sometimes you go through different trials and different things just so you can be a testimony, so you can help other people. There are days when I can feel GOD all around me and then there are days that I don't feel HIM at all. Things happened in my life that helps me to know it couldn't had been anybody but GOD that got me through. In the Bible, in the book of John 1st chapter,

1. In the beginning was the WORD, and the WORD was with GOD, and the WORD was GOD.

2. The same was in the beginning with GOD.

3. All things were made by HIM; and without HIM was not anything made that was made.

4. In HIM was life; and the life was the light of men.

5. And the light shineth in darkness; and the darkness comprehend it not.

In the bible, JESUS is GOD's Word made flesh. As I said earlier, anything you see in the Bible that's written in all capital letters, or red letters, is GOD speaking. Something that I try to do every year is read the whole bible, front to back. I always ask GOD to give me the wisdom and the understanding I need when I read it. I feel like if you read the Bible, there are stories in there that will uplift you and let you know that GOD and JESUS are real. One of my favorite stories in the Bible is the story of Elijah and the prophets of Baal.

1 Kings Chapter 18, starting at verse

25. Elijah told them to choose one bullock for themselves and dress it first for ye are many; and call on the name of your GOD's, but put no fire under it.

26. And they took the bullock which were given them, and they dressed it and they called on the name of Baal from morning even until noon, saying, oh Baal, hear us. But there was no voice, nor any that answered. And they leaped upon the altar which was made.

27. And it came to pass at noon, that Elijah mark them, and said, cry aloud for he is a God, either he is talking, or he is pursuing, or he is on a journey or pre adventure he sleeps and must be awaked.

28. And they cried aloud. And they cut themselves after their manner with knives and lancets, till the blood gushed out upon them.

29.And it came to pass, when midday was past, and they prophesied until the time of the offering of the evening sacrifice, that there was neither voice nor any to answer nor any that regarded.

30.And Elijah said unto all the people come near unto me. And all the people came near unto him. And he repaired the altar of the LORD that was broken down.

31.And Elijah took 12 Stones according to the number of tribes of the son of Jacob until whom the word of the Lord came saying, ISREAL SHALL BE THY NAME.

32.And with the stones he built an altar in the name of the LORD. And he made a trench about the altar as great as would contain 2 measures of seed.

33.And he put the wood in order and cut the bullocks in pieces and he laid him on the wood and said. Fill 4 barrels with water, and pour it on the burnt sacrifice, and on the wood.

34.And he said, do it the second time. And they did it the second time. And he said, do it the 3rd time. And they did it the 3rd time.

35.And the water ran round and about the altar and he filled the trench also with water.

36.And it came to pass at the time of the offering of the evening sacrificed, that Elijah the prophet came near, and said, LORD, GOD of Abraham, Isaac, and Israel, let it be known this day that thou art GOD in Israel, and that I am thy servant, and that I have done all these things at thy word.

37.Hear me, oh LORD, hear me, that this people may know that thou art the LORD GOD, and that thou hast turned their heart back again.

38.Then the fire of the LORD fell, and consumed the burnt sacrifice, and the wood, and the stone, and the dust, and licked up the water that was in the trench.

39.And when all the people saw it, they fell on their faces. And they said the LORD, HE is GOD, the LORD, HE is GOD.

40.And Elijah said unto them, take the prophets of Baal, let not one of them escape. And they took them, and Elijah brought them down to the brook Kishon. And slew them there.

I love that story. It tells how GOD moves. The bible is full of mysteries, love stories, action, wisdom and knowledge. Please read it all the way thru at least once.

Isaiah 41:10 FEAR THOU NOT; FOR I AM WITH THEE: BE NOT DISMAYED: FOR I AM THY GOD. I WILL STRENGTHEN THEE; YEA, I WILL HELP THEE, YEA I WILL UPHOLD THEE WITH THE RIGHT HAND OF MY RIGHTEOUSNESS.

Faith and Does GOD Hear Our Prayers?

Faith is a mighty word. It's something the Bible tells us we half to have. If you go to Matthew chapter 17 and the 20th verse it said, if you have faith as a grain of mustard seed, I don't know if any of you have ever seen a mustard seed, but they are so tiny and small. GOD is letting us know, HE's not expecting very much out of us, but we half to have faith. This verse actually reads, and JESUS said unto them, BECAUSE OF YOUR UNBELIEF: FOR VERILY I SAY UNTO YOU, IF YE HAVE FAITH AS A GRAIN OF MUSTARD SEED, YE SHALL SAY UNTO THIS MOUNTAIN, REMOVE HENCE TO YONDER PLACE; AND IT SHALL REMOVE; AND NOTHING SHALL BE IMPOSSIBLE UNTO YOU. What the disciples lacked was belief. They didn't believe they could do what JESUS does. To move something as big as a mountain, verse 21 said, HOWBEIT THIS KIND GOETH NOT OUT BUT BY PRAYER AND FASTING. JESUS is saying, this kind, (moving mountains) can be done but you, half to pray and fast. Ahhhhh fasting, A subject where a lot of people get confused. The Bible says, Matthew 6:16, MOREOVER WHEN YE FAST, BE NOT, AS THE HYPOCRITES, OF A SAD COUNTENACE: FOR THEY DISFIGURE THEIR FACES, THAT THEY MAY APPEAR UNTO MEN TO FAST. VERILY I SAY UNTO YOU, THEY HAVE THEIR REWARDS. 17.BUT THOU, WHEN THOU FASTEST, ANOINT THINE HEAD, AND WASH. I think fasting is something you and GOD should decide on how it's done. Some believe you're not suppose to eat or drink, but there are people with Medical issues that half to have water or food. I've done 3 days without water or food, but I've also done a fast where I would start at 12 am, and I wouldn't eat anything until after 12 noon. Some people say they start at night and don't eat until morning because the word breakfast means to break fast. That's why I said talk to GOD about how you should go about it. It really is between you and HIM. And I've seen in the bible where groups of people even do it. So, don't be afraid to fast, it may help. If we go to, Hebrew Chapter 11, verse 1, Now faith is the substance of things hoped for, and the evidence of things not seen. I've noticed that that word now could be a little confusing because it could just be like now faith, but what it's saying is now, which is, right now, at this moment. You, half to have faith right at that very second. You, half to believe. There's no shame if you feel like your faith is not strong enough. I usually ask GOD to help my unbelief.

Mark 9, verse 23 & 24. There was a man who brought his son to JESUS, the boy had a dumb spirit and the disciples were unable to cast out the spirit. JESUS said to the father of the boy,

23. IF THOU CANST BELIEVE, ALL THINGS ARE POSSIBLE TO HIM THAT BELIEVE. 24. And straightway the father of the child cried out, and said with tears, LORD, I believe; help thou my unbelief. So, if you ever have a little doubt, just ask GOD to help your unbelief. At least you are admitting there is a problem with your faith and your belief. GOD even said greater things we shall do in HIS name.

Matthew 21:22 says. AND ALL THINGS, WHATSOEVER YE SHALL ASK IN PRAYER, BELIEVING, YE SHALL RECEIVE. Because a lot of you don't have access to You Tube, this is the story Steve Harvey told. A man died and went to heaven and he met Peter at the gate. Peter started to escort him to see GOD and as they went, he saw all these doors with people's names on them. He said, hey Peter, what's all these doors with people's names on them. Peter told him not to worry about them but as they kept going, he saw a door with his name on it. He said, wait a minute Peter, this here door got my name on it, something Something I need to know? Peter said don't worry about it lets keep going. But the man would not move until Peter showed him what was behind the door. When Peter opened the door, there were boxes on shelves all thru the room with his name on them. He said, Peter, what's all these boxes? Peter said, that's, all, of the blessing, all, of the things GOD wanted to give to you, but,

1.you didn't ask HIM for it,

2.you didn't believe you could have it,

3.you doubted HIM,

4.then you felt like you weren't worthy.

Then he shows this cartoon of a guy leaning on a street sign called Doubt it Drive, and he says, when GOD sends your package, HE only sends it on one street, faith street. He said, you can't be on Doubt it Drive, because your package is just gone go right on thru. You can't be on, not meant to be way, cause guess what, your package is gone keep going right on by. You can't get your feeling hurt and be on I not worthy way, because that package is gone keep going right on by. You have not, because you ask not. Then you start feeling sorry for yourself and you're over there on Pity Me Way, your package gone keep right on going. If you stay, on Faith Street, don't ever get off, If, you wait on it, here it come, It, may not come when you want it, but GOD is always right on time.

If you get off, your package will return to sender and you'll have nothing. Stay on Faith St. Please family, friends, no matter what happens. KEEP YOUR FAITH! And yes, GOD does hear all, of your prayers!

Can We Really Speak Things Into Existence

This is an area where I have seen and heard so many negative people. I even saw where one guy said, it's in the bible, GOD said only HE could speak things into existence. That is so far from the truth. GOD gave everyone power to speak things into existence, JESUS even said greater things we shall do than HE did because HE will go before HIS FATHER. Every time you pray, you're speaking things into existence. You mean to tell me when you ask GOD to take care of a family member, you're not speaking it? When you ask GOD to bless you with the finances to pay your bills, you're not speaking that thing to happen? Why did you ask HIM then? Oh, ye of little faith. There's a story in the 21st Chapter of Matthew that tells us how JESUS was hungry, and he passed this fig tree and there were no figs on it. JESUS said to that fig tree, LET NO FRUIT BE ON THEE HENCEFORWARD FOR EVER. Right then and there the fig tree withered away. On the 20th verse it says and when the disciples saw it, they marveled, saying, how soon is the fig tree withered away! Now, for all you people that don't believe we can speak things into existence, JESUS can tell you we can better than I can...

Verse 21 JESUS answered and said unto them, VERILY I SAY UNTO YOU, IF YE HAVE FAITH, AND DOUBT NOT, YE SHALL NOT ONLY DO THESE THINGS WHICH IS DONE TO THE FIG TREE, BUT ALSO YE SHALL SAY (oh oh, if I say it, am I not speaking it) UNTO THIS MOUNTAIN, BE THOU REMOVED, AND BE THOU CAST INTO THE SEA; AND IT SHALL BE DONE.

22 AND ALL THINGS, WHATSOEVER YE SHALL ASK IN PRAYER, BELIEVING, YE SHALL RECEIVE.

Proverbs Chapter 18:21 Death and life are in the power of the tongue: and they that love it shall eat the fruit thereof.

After those three verses, how can you not believe that we have the power to speak things into existence. There's a true movie coming out in April about a woman who spoke her son back to life. The movie is called Breakthru.

Does GOD Give Us Dreams

Yes, HE does. Some people don't remember their dreams or even if they have had a dream. Job Chapter 33

Verses 14 & 15. For GOD speaketh once, yea twice, yet man proceiveth it not. In a dream, in a vision of the night, when deep sleep fallest upon men.

I always write my dreams down. I have had dreams, wake up and go to the bathroom, come back and go right back into the same dream. Something can wake me up again and I'll go right back into the same dream the 3rd time, so whenever that happens, I know that that dream came from GOD, because how can you go to sleep 3 times and still go back into the same dream. But when a dream that I've had happens, I always say, wow dejavu. Some of my dreams are not always sunshine and rainbows (good). I have had dreams where I'm being chased by the devil. He never catches me but he's far enough behind me where I can see him. When I was young, even now, I have a lot of dreams about tornadoes. They always come about a half mile away from me and then goes back up. Another thing I'm always being chased by in my dreams is a T-rex. SO, telling you that scripture in the book of Job should prove GOD gives us dreams. HE said it, LOL, I didn't.

Does Angels or Ghost Exist

I would say yes on both accounts I don't believe in monsters under the bed or monsters in the closet, but in my time, I have seen and heard a lot of weird and strange things. When you walk into my mom's home, you may hear a little girl laugh, even when we knew there wasn't anyone in the house. Just about all of us had heard her. One of my sisters said she went upstairs and turned right in the hallway and there was a big tall Indian standing there, and then there was Elizabeth. Before we moved in the house, the people that used to live there told my mom about a little white girl who had killed herself in the basement. And then one day my nephew was in one of the bedrooms, half sleep, and this little girl came out of the closet. She said her name was Elizabeth and then told him how she had killed herself in the basement. He never told anybody that story until one day he decided to tell me. Because by this time I had seen and heard enough spirits to know they were real.

2. Two weeks after my daughter Tiffany had passed away, my other daughter Tammy and I had just got home from the store. I opened the door with my arms full of bags and headed for the kitchen. When I turned the corner there was a female standing there with a pair of red sweatpants on. I set the groceries down. I remember saying in my mind, why isn't Tammy helping me bring the groceries in the house and right when I thought that, the person turned and went into the basement. I turned and I was fussing in my mind, I said I can't believe Tammy went into the basement and she knew I needed help getting the groceries in the house. I turned that corner and pulled on the door and almost ran into Tammy and I still hadn't put 2 and 2 together that someone was standing by the stove and had just went into the basement. It wasn't until years later, after I had moved out of the house that I realized that was Tiffany standing there and she went into the basement because she had a shop where she did hair down there. There was a door down in the basement, but you couldn't get thru it because it was nailed shut.

3. I was over to my son's house one day babysitting my grandkids, and my grandbaby Alayah, who was 4 at the time, and was born

way after Tiffany had passed away, said, who's that, she pointed over my head. I said who? She said that. I said I don't know. She said well she looks like Tammy. I said, must be my daughter Tiffany that passed away. And when I told my son about it, he said she had mentioned tiffany's name before, and he had never told her about Tiffany. That had been a year before the other incident. Just about all, of my family, kids and adults, has seen spirits in moms house.

4.One day I was at this church, and I was playing the drums, and they had this man lying on the floor and there was about 3 or 4 people around him praying that this demon would come out of him. This went on for a while and finally I looked down at the man and when I did this demon looking face looked up at me and started laughing. When I left, the lady that I brought asked me if I had seen that demons face laughing and I told her, Yep I did.

5.One day I was over to my sister's house and her great grand baby, Whom, is artistic, was in this room down the hall playing and laughing with his invisible friend. The way he was laughing and playing you could tell there was somebody there with him and he wasn't alone.

6.But Not all spirits that I have encountered were good. I remember one night, my daughter Tiffany and I were at the house, she was half sleep, but she was still talking to me. She finally dozed off and I dozed off. Something shook me awake and when it did, I looked over at my daughter and there was this black thing hovering over her and I shouted, hey, and it took off running and went right through the wall in the living room.

7.When my daughter Tiffany was in the hospital, two days before she passed away, Mother Grayson and Aunt Fanny was there with her and she asked Mother to fix her some greens, sweet potatoes, mac and cheese and a peach cobbler. She said she would do it the next day, but Tiff said, you half to fix it today, because I may not be here tomorrow. Then she asked if they saw the two men sitting across the room who came to get her. They said no. Mother didn't make it back, but that night she died. The two men were angels.

8.My mom also told me the story of how another family member was laying on his bed, and when some of the family came into the room, he told them of how two men were looking in his window and told him they were going to get the lady across the street and then come back and get him. At that time someone came in and told them the lady across the street had died. They went over to her home but when they came back he had died also. Just as the angels had told him.

9.Last, I want to tell you about these things called witch riders. If you go to the Dream Studies Portal web site, they called it Sleep Paralysis or witch riders. What happens is, you feel like you're being held down and can't move or get up. When I was younger, I looked it up in the dictionary and it said that you could tell when witch riders had been messing with horses because they would braid the horse's hair in different spots. But recently I looked up the word on my cell phone and they decided they wanted to connect them with all African American people only. They say they are these things that come when you're caught between being sleep and awake. You can't move at all. But you can hear everything that's happening around you real loud and you try and try to move but you can't. You think you see what's going on around you but it's not true. There was one time when I had this real big tarantula looking spider crawling up my chest, I couldn't move to knock it off but when these things happen, and you call on the name of JESUS, then it can break whatever is holding you down.

The Bible tells us in Ephesians, chapter 10, verse 12, for we wrestle not against flesh and blood, but against principalities, against power, against the rulers of the darkness of this world, against spiritual wickedness in high places.

. Hebrew chapter 13 verse 2 said be not forgetful to entertain strangers, for there by some have entertained Angels unawares. When Re'Kole and Ne'Kole were younger, they used to sleep on the 3rd floor. Ne'Kole said she woke up one night and there was this glowing white figure standing over her bed. She said she just pulled the sheet over her head, turned over and went back to sleep. I remember onetime Ne'kole was in the kitchen with Re'Kole. Re'Kole came out. I was sleep, but I heard this noise coming out of the kitchen. I got up and went in there and Ne'Kole was choking. I know that was an angel that woke me up at that moment to save her life.

GOD allows us to call on angels for help, we have help angels, healing angels, finance angels, message angels, mechanical angels, even angels that fight wars and battles for us. Learn how to use your angels. GOD allows us to use them for help. Try looking up the word angel in your bible's concordance. There are many stories about them and things they did in the Bible. GOD will send you an angel. Even in Death. Psalms 23rd chapter says, they comforted me!

I always worried about my mom when I was little and at school. My mom said one day she woke up and I was sitting on the end of her bed. She asked me why I wasn't at school, and she said I got up and went into the closet in the other room. She said she followed me but when she looked in there I was gone. I think because I always asked GOD to watch over my mother, HE sent and angel just to do that. I also think it looked like me so my mom would not be afraid. She also told me a story about how she used to worry about her kids at school. She said she would always pray and ask GOD to please take care of her kids. She said one day she saw a vision of this big white dog, it wrapped itself around all of her kids. She said when she asked GOD about it, HE said, DO I NOT TAKE CARE OF THAT WHICH IS MINE. Want to do something to help you believe, watch the tv show It's a Miracle or Touched By An Angel. Those 2 will really help your unbelief.

Is Prophecy Real

In life you will always find naysayers and people who don't believe and don't want you to believe because of things that happened in their life. Prophecy is real, And GOD can send a child, a friend, someone you don't know, even a drunk person to prophesied to you. If GOD gives me a word for you, I'm going to come and tell you and it's up to you to accept what I say. GOD can send messages, help, good news, and peace, even a warning to you through other people. I'm not bragging or boasting, but GOD has used me to tell people different things, even warnings, and people have come back and told me that what GOD gave me to tell them happened. One thing I always ask GOD is to allow me to prophesy not prop-a- lie. let me give you a couple of scriptures in the bible where it lets you know that prophecy is real. The first scripture is 1st Thessalonians 5th chapter, 20th verse, which says, Despise not prophesying.

Jeremiah 1: 7 & 8 & 9b

7. But the LORD said unto me, SAY NOT, I AM A CHILD: FOR THOU SHALT GO TO ALL THAT I WILL SEND THEE, AND WHATSOEVER I COMMAND THEE THOU SHALT SPEAK.

8. BE NOT AFRAID OF THEIR FACES: FOR I AM WITH THEE, saith the LORD.

9b. BEHOLD, I HAVE PUT MY WORDS IN THY MOUTH.

What I think I'll do is just quote to you all the gifts of the spirit, which is given to you from GOD; Because you need to know that prophesy is not the only gift that GOD will give you. I'm coming to you from the 12th chapter of 1st Corinthian's, and I'm going to type to you the 1st thru the 11th verse.

1.Now concerning spiritual gifts, brethren, I would not have you ignorant.

2.You know that you were Gentiles, carried away unto these dumb idols, even as you were led.

3.Wherefore I give you to understand, that no man speaking by the spirit of GOD calleth JESUS accursed; and that no man can say that JESUS is the LORD, but by the HOLY GHOST.

4.Now there are diversities of gifts, but the same spirit.

5.And there are differences of administrations, but the same LORD.

6.And there are diversities of operations, but it is the same GOD which worketh all in all.

7.But the manifestation of the Spirit is given to every man to profit withal.

8.For to one is given by the Spirit the word of wisdom; to another the word of knowledge by the same Spirit.

9.To another faith by the same Spirit; to another the gifts of healing by the same Spirit:

10. To another the working of miracles; to another prophecy; to another discerning of Spirits: to another diver's kinds of tongues: to another the interpretations of tongues:

11. But all these worketh that one and the selfsame Spirit, dividing to every man severally as HE (GOD) will. These are things that I like to say (laughing) that GOD would do for you, when you are wrapped up, tide up, tangled up in GOD. When you can get past the point of unbelief and doubt you will see the things that GOD can do for you. I am a strong, stand on my faith, praying person. If you would like for me to pray for you. Email me at blessedoneat65@hotmail.com We will push your prayer. (Pray Until Something Happens...push)

This is very important for you to understand, if GOD, HIMSELF, gives you something, keep with what HE says to you. I don't care if I come to you and say an Angel told me to tell you to do what GOD told you to do, or not to do, don't listen to me, listen to GOD. To understand more of what I'm saying please go to 1st King, 13th chapter and read the whole story. You know what, just in case you don't own a bible (that should make you run out and get one). I'll type the 6th thru the 24th verse. Now doing so should make you want to read the whole 13th Chapter, so go buy a bible!

Verse 6. And the King answered and said unto the man of GOD, intreat now the face of the LORD thy GOD, and pray for me, that my hand may be, restored me again. And the man of GOD besought the LORD, and the king's hand, restored him again, and became as it was before.

7. And the King said unto the man of GOD, come home with me and refreshed thyself, and I will give thee a reward.

8. And the man of GOD said unto the King, if thou wilt give me half thine house, I will not go in with thee, neither will I eat bread nor drink water in this place.

9. For so, it was, charged me by the word of the LORD, saying, EAT NO BREAD, NOR DRINK WATER, NOR TURN AGAIN BY THE SAME WAY THAT THOU CAMETH.

10. So he went another way, and returned not by the way that he came to Beth-el.

11. Now there dwelled an old prophet in Beth-el; and his sons came and told him all the works that the man of GOD had done that day in Beth-el: the words which he had spoken unto the King, them they told also to their father.

12. And their father said unto them, what way went he? For his sons had seen what way the man of GOD went from Judah.

13. And he said unto his sons, saddle me the ass. So, they saddled him the ass: and he rode there on.

14. And he went after the man of GOD. And found him sitting under an oak: and he said unto him. Art thou the man of GOD, that camest from Judah? and he said, I am.

15. Then he said unto him. Come home with me, an eat bread.

16. And he said, I may not return with thee, nor go in with thee, neither will I eat bread nor drink water with thee in this place.

17. For it was said to me by the word of the LORD, THOU SHALL EAT NO BREAD NOR DRINK WATER THERE, NOR TURN AGAIN TO GO BY THE WAY THAT THOU CAMEST.

 18. He said unto him, I am a prophet also as thou art, and an angel spake unto me by the word of the LORD, saying, bring him back with thee into thine house, that he may eat bread and drink water. But he lied unto him.

19. So he went back with him, and did eat bread in his house, and drink water.

20. And it came to pass as they sit at the table, that the word of the LORD came unto the prophet that brought him back.

21. And he cried unto the man of GOD that came from Judah, saying, thus said the LORD, FORASMUCH AS THOU HAST DISOBEYED THE MOUTH OF THE LORD, AND HAST NOT KEPT THE COMMANDMENT WHICH THE LORD THY GOD COMMANDED THEE,

22. BUT CAMEST BACK, AND HAST EATEN BREAD AND DRUNK WATER IN THE PLACE, OF THE WHICH THE LORD DID SAY TO THEE, EAT NO BREAD, AND DRINK NO WATER; THY CARCASE SHALL NOT COME UNTO THE SEPULCHRE OF THY FATHERS.

23. And it came to pass, after he had eaten bread, and after he had drunk, that he saddled for him the ass, to wit, for the prophet he had brought back.

24. And when he was gone, a lion met him by the way, and slew him: and his carcass was cast in the way, and the ass stood by it, the lion also stood by the carcass.

So, by reading this, if GOD HIMSELF tells you to do something, listen to every word and please do it. And please don't do what anyone else says, no matter what!

Bullies

Bullies come in all ages, shapes and sizes. Even your own parents can be considered bullies. You have to listen to everything and almost every word your parents say, because they are your parents, and the bible says: Exodus chapter 20th verse 12 HONOUR THY FATHER AND THY MOTHER: THAT THY DAYS MAY BE LONG UPON THE LAND WHICH THE LORD THY GOD GIVETH THEE. You listen but you don't have to take it in when they start calling you names, or telling you that you're dumb and you'll never amount to anything, you don't have to listen to that or keep it in your mind or your heart. Parents, there are scriptures in the bible that allows you to know that you're not suppose, to hurt your children in any form, shape or fashion. Ephesians chapter 6 verses 1-4 says.

1.Children, obey your parents in the LORD: for this is right.

2.HONOR THY FATHER AND MOTHER; which is the first commandment with promise.

3.THAT IT MAY BE WELL WITH THEE, AND THOU MAYEST LIVE LONG ON THE EARTH.

4.And ye fathers, (and mothers) provoke not your children to wrath: but bring them up in the nurture and admonition of the LORD.

Colossians 3:18 & 19 and 21

18.Wives, submit yourselves unto your OWN husbands, as it is fit in the LORD.

19.Husbands, love YOUR wives, and be not bitter against them.

21.Fathers, (mothers) provoke not your children to anger, lest they be discouraged.

How come your wife, or husband was good enough to marry, but not good enough to treat right. Some of you stood in a church, and said I will love you thru sickness and health, thru ups and downs, till death do us part? Then the minute the devil sends someone to break up your marriage, make you think that person is the best thing since sliced bread, you're ready to leave them. Then, if you end up marrying that person, your marriage is worse than the first marriage. The devil makes it that way, it's his job to kill, steal and destroy your marriage. And please, stop running after people for looks and what they might have. GOD really does have someone for you. They may take a while to come, but please let GOD handle your love life. I tell people to watch that movie called Bedazzled with Brandon Fraser and Elizabeth Hurley. It's a good movie about this guy that wanted this lady so bad, the devil stepped in. Ok, back to bullies. There are several reasons why a child or person can be a bully, it could be they're hurting, or something's not right at home, or somebody's teasing them, or their parents are abusive. My favorite, their jealous of you. To me, there are a lot of ugly ducklings in this world that turn into very beautiful Swans. I don't care who they are, or who you are, don't let what other people say to you, or do to you, sway you, or make you want to take your own life. No one, but GOD and you have control over your life. Just remember the problem is not you, it's them. Parents, please stop saying hurtful things to your kids, instead talk to them about bullies and how cruel some people can be. Ask your kids if they're being bullied and then either talk to their teacher, the principal or to their parent. There are too many kids taking their own lives or shooting up schools because of bullies, don't let your child be one of them. Also, find out if your child is a bully. We need to stop the bullies in this world. By setting an example. If you don't want it done to your kids, stop your kids from doing it. Bullies usually are kids that are hurting, stop the hurt please. Help a child that is a bully, find out why they do it. You'd be surprised, all they wanted in the first place was someone to help them or talk to them about a problem they were having. Don't be a bully! Be a blessing! I know it may be hard when the president is America's biggest bully!

My Favorite Promises and Scriptures From GOD

Old Testament

1. 1 Chronicles 4:10

And Jabez called on the GOD of Israel, saying, oh that thou wouldest bless me indeed, and enlarge my coast, and that thine hand might be with me, and that thou wouldest keep me from evil, that it may not grieve me! And GOD granted him that which he requested.

2. Psalms 23

The LORD is my Shepherd: I shall not want. HE maketh me to lie down in the green pastures: HE leadeth me beside the still waters. He restores my soul: he leadeth me in the paths of righteousness for HIS name sake. Yea though I walk through the valley of the shadow of death, I will fear no evil, for THOU art with me, THY rod, THY staff, they comfort me. THOU prepareth a table before me in the presence of mine enemies. THOU anointed my head with oil, my Cup runneth over. Surely, goodness and mercy shall follow me all the days of my life: and I should dwell in the house of the LORD forever.

3. Exodus 20: 1-17

1. And GOD spoke all these words, saying.

2. I AM THE LORD THY GOD WHICH HAVE BROUGHT THEE OUT OF THE LAND OF EGYPT, OUT OF THE HOUSE OF BONDAGE.

3. THOU SHALT HAVE NO OTHER GODS BEFORE ME.

4. THOU SHALT NOT MAKE UNTO THEE ANY GRAVEN IMAGE OF ANY LIKENESS OF ANYTHING THAT IS IN THE HEAVENS ABOVE, OR THAT IS IN THE EARTH BENEATH, OR THAT IS IN THE WATERS UNDER THE EARTH.

5. THOU SHALL NOT BOW DOWN THYSELF TO THEM, NOR SERVE THEM. FOR I THE LORD THY GOD AM A JEALOUS GOD. VISITING THE INIQUITY OF THE FATHERS UPON THE CHILDREN UMTO THE THIRD AND FORTH GENERATIONS OF THEM THAT HATE ME;

6. AND SHOWING MERCY UNTO THOUSANDS OF THEM THAT LOVE ME AND KEEP MY   COMMANDMENTS.

7. THOU SHALT NOT TAKE THE NAME OF THE LORD, THY GOD IN VAIN: FOR THE LORD WILL NOT HOLD HIM GUILTLESS THAT TAKETH HIS NAME IN VAIN.

8. REMEMBER THE SABBATH DAY, TO KEEP IT HOLY,

9. SIX DAYS SHALT THOU LABOUR, AND DO ALL THY WORK:

10. BUT THE SEVENTH DAY IS THE SABBATH OF THE LORD THY GOD. IN IT THY SHALT NOT DO ANY WORK, THY, NOR THY SON, NOR THY DAUGHTER, THY MANSERVANT, NOR THY MAIDSERVANT, NOR THY CATTLE, NOR THY STRANGER THAT IS WITHIN THY GATES:

11. FOR IN SIX DAYS THE LORD MADE HEAVEN AND EARTH, THE SEA, AND ALL THAT IN THEM IS, AND RESTED THE SEVENTH DAY: WHEREFOR THE LORD BLESSED THE SEVENTH DAY AND HOLLOWED IT.

12. HONOR THY FATHER AND THY MOTHER THAT THY DAYS MAY BE LONG UPON THE LAND WHICH THE LORD THY GOD GIVETH THEE.

13. THOU SHALT NOT KILL.

14. THOU SHALT NOT COMMIT ADULTERY.

15. THOU SHALT NOT STEAL.

16. THOU SHALT NOT BEAR FALSE WITNESS AGAINST THY NEIGHBOUR.

17. THOU SHALT NOT COVET THY NEIGHBOUR'S HOUSE, THY SHALT NOT COVET THY NEIGHBOUR'S WIFE, NOR HIS MANSERVANT, NOR HIS MAIDSERVANT, NOR HIS OX, NOR HIS ASS, NOR ANYTHING THAT IS THY NEIGHBOURS.

4. Numbers 23:19

GOD is not a man, that HE should lie: neither the son of man, that HE should repent: has HE not said, and shall HE not do it? Or has HE spoken, and shall HE not make good?

5. Deuteronomy 1:11

The LORD GOD of your fathers make you a thousand times so many more as you are and bless you as HE has promised you!

6. 2 Chronicles 7:14

IF MY PEOPLE, WHICH ARE CALLED BY NAME, SHALL HUMBLE THEMSELVES, AND PRAY, AND SEEK MY FACE, AND TURN FROM

THEIR WICKED WAYS: THEN WILL I HEAR FROM HEAVEN AND WILL FORGIVE THEIR SINS, AND WILL HEAL THEIR LAND.

7. Psalms 121:1-8

1. I will lift, up mine eyes into the hills which cometh my help.

2. My help comes from the LORD which made heaven and earth.

3. HE will not suffer thy foot to be moved: HE that keepeth thee will not slumber.

4. Behold, HE that keepeth Israel, shall neither slumber nor sleep.

5. The LORD is thy keeper: The LORD is thy shade upon thy right hand.

6. The sun shall not smite thee by day, nor the moon by night.

7. The LORD shall preserve thee from all evil: HE shall preserve thy soul.

8. The LORD shall preserve thy going out and thy coming in from this time forth, and even for evermore.

8. Deuteronomy 6:10 & 11

10. And it shall be, when the LORD thy GOD shall have brought thee into the land which HE sware unto thy fathers, to Abraham, to Isaac, and Jacob, to give thee great and goodly cities, which thou buildedst not,

11. And houses full of all good things which thy filledst not, wells digged, which thy diggest not, vineyards and olive trees which thou planet not: when thou shall have eaten and be full.

9. Joshua 1: 8 & 9

THIS BOOK OF THE LAW SHALL NOT DEPART OUT OF THY MOUTH; BUT THOU SHALT MEDITATE THEREIN DAY AND NIGHT, THAT THOU MAYEST OBSERVE TO DO ACCORDING TO ALL THAT IS WRITTEN THEREIN: FOR THEN THOU SHALT MAKE THY WAY PROPEROUS AND THEN THOU SHALT HAVE GOOD SUCCESS.

9. HAVE NOT I COMMANDED THEE? BE STRONG AND OF GOOD COURAGE: BE NOT AFRAID. NEITHER BE THOU DISMAYED: FOR THE LORD THY GOD IS WITH THEE WHITHER-SOEVER THOU GOEST.

10. Psalms 35

Plead my cause, O LORD, with them that strive with me; fight against them that fight against me.

11. Psalms 37: 4 & 5

4. Delight thyself also in the LORD, and he shall give thee the desires of thine heart.

5. Commit thy way unto the LORD; trust also in HIM; and HE shall bring it to pass.

12. Psalms 37:25

I have been young, now I am old, yet have I not seen the righteous forsaken, nor HIS seed begging bread.

13. Psalms 91

1. He that dwelleth in the secret place of the most, High, shall abide under the shadow of the Almighty.

2. I will say of the LORD HE is my refuge and my fortress: my GOD; in HIM will I trust

3. Surely, HE shall deliver thee from the snare of the fowler, and from the noisome pestilence.

4 HE shall cover thee with his feathers, and under HIS wings shall thou trust: HIS truth shall be thy shield and buckler.

5. Thy shall not be afraid for the terror by night: nor for the arrow that flieth by day.

6. Nor the pestilence that walketh in darkness; nor for the destruction that wasteth at noonday.

7. A thousand shall fall at thy side, and 10,000 at thy right hand; but it shall not come nigh thee.

8. Only with thine eyes shalt thou behold see the reward of the wicked.

9. Because thou hast made the LORD, which is my refuge, even the most, High, thy habitation.

10. There shall no evil befall the, neither shall any plague come nigh thy dwelling.

11. For HE shall give HIS angels charge over thee, to keep thee in all thy ways.

12. They shall bear thee up in their hands, lest thou dash thy foot against a stone.

13. Thou shalt tread upon the lion and adder: the young lion and dragon shalt thou trample under feet.

14. BECAUSE HE HALT SET HIS LOVE UPON ME, THEREFORE WILL I DELIVER HIM: I WILL SET HIM ON HIGH, BECAUSE HE HALT KNOWN MY NAME.

15. HE SHALL CALL UPON ME, AND I WILL ANSWER HIM: I WILL BE WITH HIM IN TROUBLE; I WILL DELIVER HIM, AND HONOUR HIM.

16. WITH LONG LIFE WILL I SATISFY HIM: AND SHEW HIM MY SALVATION

14. Proverbs 3: 5 & 6

5. Trust in the LORD with all thine heart; and lean not unto thine own understanding.

6. In all thy ways acknowledge HIM, and HE shall direct thy path.

15. Proverbs 10:22

The blessings of the LORD, it maketh rich, and HE addeth no sorrow with it.

16. Proverbs 13:22

A good man leaveth an inheritance to his children's children: and the wealth of the sinner is laid up for the just.

17. Proverb 18: 16

A man's gift maketh room for him, and bringest him before great men.

18. Proverbs 18:22

Whoso findest a wife findest a good thing, and obtainest favor of the LORD.

19. Proverb 18:24

A man that hath friends must shew himself friendly: and there is a friend that sticks closer than a brother.

20. Isaiah 40:31

But they that wait upon the LORD shall renew their strength; they shall mount up on wings as an eagle's, they shall run, and not be weary; and they shall walk and not faint.

21. Jeremiah 1: 4 & 5

4.Then the word of the LORD came unto me, saying,

5. BEFORE I FORMED THEE IN THE BELLY, I KNEW THEE; AND BEFORE THOU CAMEST FORTH OUT OF THE WOMB I SANCTIFIED THEE, AND I ORDAINED THEE A PROPHET UNTO THE NATIONS.

22. Joel 2:25

AND I WILL RESTORE TO YOU THE YEARS THAT THE LOCUST HATH EATEN. THE CANKERWORM, AND THE CATERPILLAR, AND THE PALMERWORM, MY GREAT ARMY WHICH I SENT AMONG YOU.

23. Habakkuk 2:2

Write the vision.

24. Malachi 3: 10-12

10.BRING YE ALL THE TITHES INTO THE STOREHOUSE, THAT THERE MAY BE MEAT IN MINE HOUSE, AND PROVE ME NOW HEREWITH, saith the LORD of host. IF I WILL NOT OPEN YOU THE WINDOWS OF HEAVEN, AND POUR YOU OUT

A BLESSING, THAT THERE SHALL NOT BE ROOM ENOUGH TO RECEIVE IT.

11. AND I WILL REBUKE THE DEVOURER FOR YOUR SAKE, AND HE SHALL NOT DESTROY THE FRUITS OF YOUR GROUND; NEITHER SHALL YOUR VINE CAST HER FRUIT BEFORE THE TIME IN THE FIELD, saith the LORD of host.

12. AND ALL NATIONS SHALL CALL YOU BLESSED: FOR YE SHALL BE A DELIGHTSOME LAND, saith the LORD of host.

New Testament

Matthew 5:3-12

3. BLESSED ARE THE POOR IN SPIRIT: FOR THEIRS IS THE KINGDOM OF HEAVEN.
4. BLESSED ARE THEY THAT MOURN: FOR THEY SHALL BE COMFORTED.
5. BLESSED ARE THE MEEK: FOR THEY SHALL INHERIT THE EARTH.
6. BLESSED ARE THEY WHICH DO HUNGER AND THRIST AFTER RIGHTEOUSNESS: FOR THEY SHALL BE FILLED.
7. BLESSED ARE THE MERCIFUL: FOR THEY SHALL OBTAIN MERCY.

8. BLESSED ARE THE PURE IN HEART: FOR THEY SHALL SEE GOD.

9. BLESSED ARE THE PEACEMAKERS: FOR THEY SHALL BE CALLED THE CHILDREN OF GOD.

10.   BLESSED ARE THEY WHICH ARE PERSCUTED FOR RIGHTEOUSNESS SAKE: FOR THEIRS IS THE KINGDOM OF HEAVEN.

11.   BLESSED ARE YE WHEN MEN SHALL REVILE YOU, AND PERSCUTE YOU, AND SHALL SAY ALL MANNER OF EVIL AGAINST YOU FALSELY, FOR MY SAKE.

12.   REJOICE, AND BE EXCEEDIND GLAD: FOR GREAT IS YOUR REWARD IN HEAVEN: FOR SO PERSECUTED THEY THE PROPHETS WHICH WERE BEFORE YOU.

2. Matthew 17:18-21

18. And JESUS rebuke the devil, and he departed out of him, and the child was cured from that very hour.

19. Then came the disciples to JESUS apart and said, why could not we cast him out?

20. And JESUS said unto them, BECAUSE OF YOUR UNBELIEF: FOR VERILY I SAY UNTO YOU, IF YE HAD FAITH AS A GRAIN OF MUSTARD SEED, YE SHALL SAY UNTO THIS MOUNTAIN, REMOVE HENCE TO YOUNDER PLACE; AND IT SHALL BE REMOVE; AND NOTHING SHALL BE IMPOSIBLE UNTO YOU.

21. HOWBEIT THIS KIND GOETH NOT OUT BUT BY PRAYER AND FASTING.

3.Matthew 21:21 & 22

21. JESUS answered and said unto them, VERILY I SAY UNTO YOU, IF YE HAVE FAITH, AND DOUBT NOT, YE SHALL NOT ONLY DO THIS WHICH IS DONE TO THE FIG TREE, BUT SLSO IF YE SHALL SAY UNTO THIS MOUNTAIN, BE THOU REMOVED, AND BE THOU CAST INTO THE SEA; IT SHALL BE DONE.

22. AND ALL THINGS WHATSOEVER YE SHALL ASK IN PRAYER, BELIEVING, YE SHALL RECEIVE.

4. John 14:11-15

11. BELIEVE ME THAT I AM IN THE FATHER, AND THE FATHER IN ME: OR ELSE BELIEVE ME FOR THE VERY WORKS SAKE.

12. VERILY, VERILY I SAY UNTO YOU, HE THAT BELIEVETH ON ME, THE WORKS THAT I DO SHALL HE DO ALSO; AND GREATER WORKS THAN THESE SHALL HE DO; BECAUSE I GO UNTO MY FATHER.

13. AND WHATSOEVER YE SHALL ASK

IN MY NAME, THAT WILL I DO, THAT THE FATHER MAY BE GLORIFIED IN THE SON.

14. IF YE SHALL ASK ANYTHING IN MY NAME, I WILL DO IT.

15. IF YOU LOVE ME, KEEP MY COMMANDMENTS.

5. Romans 9:38 & 39

38. For I am persuaded, that neither death, nor life, nor angels, nor principalities, nor powered, nor present, nor things to come.

39. Nor height, nor depth, nor any other creature, shall be able to separate us from the love of GOD, which is in CHRIST JESUS our LORD.

6. 1 Corinthians 6:9 & 10

9.Know ye not that the unrighteous shall not inherit the Kingdom of GOD? Be not deceived: neither fornicators, nor idolaters, nor adulterers, nor effeminate, nor abusers of themselves with mankind.

10.Nor thieves, nor covetous, nor drunkards, nor revilers, nor extortioners, shall inherit the Kingdom of GOD.

7. 1 Corinthians 13:1 & 2

1. Though I speak with the tongues of men and of angels, and have not charity, I am become as sounding brass, or a tinkling cymbal.

2. And though I have the gift of prophecy, and understand all mysteries, and all knowledge, and though I have all faith, So, that I can remove mountains, and have not charity, I am nothing.

8. 2 Corinthians 12:7-10

7.And lest I should be exalted above measure through the abundance of the revelation, there was given to me a thorn in the flesh, the messenger of Satan to buffet me, lest I should be exalted above measure.

8. For this thing I besought the LORD thrice, that it might depart from me.

9. And HE said unto me, MY GRACE IS SUFFICIENT FOR THEE. FOR MY STRENGTH IS MADE PERFECT IN WEAKNESS. Most gladly therefore would I rather glory in my infirmities, that the power of CHRIST may rest upon me.

10. Therefore I take pleasure in infirmity's, in reproaches, in necessities, in persecutions, in distress for CHRIST's sake: For when I am weak, then am I strong.

9. Ephesians 6:10-18

10.Finally, my brethren, be strong in the LORD and in the power of HIS might.

11. Put on the whole armor of GOD, that ye may be able to stand against the wiles of the devil.

12. For we wrestle not against flesh and blood, but against principalities, against powers, against the rulers of the darkness of this world, against spiritual wickedness in high places.

13.Wherefore take unto you the whole armor of GOD, that ye may be able to withstand in the evil day. And having done all to stand.

14. Stand therefore, having your loins girt about with truth, and having on the breastplate of righteousness:

15. And your feet shod with the preparation of the gospel of peace.

16. Above all, taking the shield of faith, wherewith Ye shall be able to quench all the fiery darts of the wicked.

17. And take the helmet of salvation, and the sword of the spirit, which is the WORD of GOD.

18. Praying always with all prayer and supplication's in the Spirit and watching thereunto with all perseverance and supplications for all saints.

10. 2 Timothy 1:7

For GOD has not given us the spirit of fear, but of power, and of love, and of a sound mind.

11. Hebrews 11:1-3

1.Now faith is the substance of things hope for, the evidence of things not seen.

2. For by it the elders obtained a good report.

3. Through faith we understand that the worlds were framed by the word of GOD, so that things which are seen were not made of things which do appear.

12. Hebrews 11:6

But without faith it is impossible to please HIM; for he that cometh to GOD must believe that HE is, and that HE is a rewarder of them that diligently seek HIM.

13.James 1:2-8

2.My brethren, count it all joy when you fall into diverse temptations.

3. Knowing this that the trying of your faith worketh patience.

4.But let patience have her perfect work, that ye may be perfect an entire, wanting nothing.

5.If any of you lack wisdom, let him ask of GOD, that giveth to all men liberally, an upbraideth not; and it shall be given him.

6. But let him ask in faith, nothing wavering. For he that wavereth is like the wave of the sea driven with the wind and tossed.

7.For let not that man think that he shall receive anything of the LORD.

8.A double minded man is unstable in all his ways.

14.James 5:13-16

13.Is any among you afflicted? Let him pray. Is any merry? Let him sing psalms.

14. Is any sick among you? Let him call for the elders of the church; anointing him with oil in the name of the LORD.

15. And the prayer of faith shall save the sick, and the LORD shall raise him up; and if he has committed sin, they shall be, forgiven him.

16. Confess your faults one to another, and pray one for another, that you may be healed. The effectual fervent prayer of a righteous man availeth much.

14.1 Peter 5:5-8

5.Likewise, year younger, submit yourselves unto the elders. Yea, all of you be subject one to another, and be clothed with humility. For GOD resisteth the proud, and giveth grace to the humble.

6. Humble yourself therefore under the mighty hand of GOD, that HE may exalt you in due time.

7. Casting all your care upon HIM; for HE cared for you.

8.Be sober, be vigilant, because your adversary the devil as a roaring lion, walketh about, seeking whom he may devour.

15. Isaiah 65:24

AND IT SHALL COME TO PASS, THAT BEFORE THEY CALL, I WILL ANSWER; AND WHILE THEY ARE YET SPEKING, I WILL HEAR.

16. Jeremiah 29:13

AND YE SHALL SEEK ME, AND FIND ME, WHEN YE SHALL SEARCH FOR ME WITH ALL YOUR HEART.

17. Jeremiah 32:27

BEHOLD, I AM THE LORD, THE GOD OF ALL FLESH: IS THERE ANYTHING TOO HARD FOR ME?

18. Matthew 7:7 & 8

7. ASK, AND IT SHALL BE GIVEN YOU; SEEK AND YOU SHALL FIND; KNOCK, AND IT SHALL BE OPEN UNTO YOU.

8. FOR EVERYONE THAT ASKETH RECEIVETH; AND HE THAT SEEKETH FINDETH; AND TO HIM THAT KNOCKETH, IT SHALL BE OPENED.

19. Matthew 18:18-20

18. VERILY I SAY UNTO YOU, WHATSOEVER YE SHALL BIND ON EARTH SHALL BE BOUND IN HEAVEN: AND WHATSOEVER YE SHALL LOOSE ON EARTH SHALL BE LOOSED IN HEAVEN.

19. AGAIN I SAY UNTO YOU, THAT IF TWO OF YOU SHALL AGREE ON EARTH AS TOUCHING, ANYTHING THAT THEY SHALL ASK, IT SHALL BE DONE FOR THEM OF MY FATHER WHICH IS IN HEAVEN.

20. FOR WHERE TWO OR THREE ARE GATHERED TOGETHER IN MY NAME, THERE AM I IN THE MIST OF THEM.

20.Matthew 24:35

HEAVEN AND EARTH SHALL PASS AWAY, BUT MY WORDS SHALL NOT PASS AWAY.

21. Matthew 6:9-13

9. AFTER THIS MANNER THEREFORE PRAY YE: OUR FATHER WHICH ART IN HEAVEN, HALLOWED BE THY NAME.

10. THY KINGDOM COME, THY WILL BE DONE IN EARTH, AS IT IS IN HEAVEN.

11. GIVE US THIS DAY OUR DAILY BREAD.

12. AND FORGIVE US OUR DEBTS, AS WE FORGIVE OUR DEBTORS.

13.AND LEAD US NOT INTO TEMPTATION. BUT DELIVER US FROM EVIL: FOR THINE IS THE KINGDOM, AND THE POWER, AND THE GLORY, FOR EVER. AMEN

What the Bible Says About...

We half to remember in this day and time the people are the ones that made unicorns and Santa magical, but the Bible speaks of these things. Also, Satyrs and Dragons. Read the Bible, I'll give you the scriptures of where it's located. The things that I'm about to say a lot of people will not believe unless they read it for themselves so that's why I'm give you what I'm about to talk about and where it can be found in the Bible.

Unicorns

Deuteronomy 33:17 His glory is like the firstling of his flock, and his horns are like the horns of unicorns: with them he shall push the people together to the end of the earth:

Psalms 22:21 Save me from the lion's mouth: for thou hast heard me from the horns of the unicorn.

Psalms 29:6 He maketh them also to skip like a calf: Lebanon and Sirion like a young unicorn.

Psalms 92:10 But my horn shalt thou exalt like the horn of a unicorn: I shall be anointed with fresh oil.

Isaiah 34:7 And the unicorns shall come down with them, and the bullocks with the bulls.

Aliens

On this subject, back in the 70s, the Royals were playing the World Series game and I looked up and there was this big round circle, with these different colors lights going in a circle around it, it looked like it was watching the game for a few second, but as quick as it came it left. I have some family members that were in Colorado's desert and they said one pulled up behind them and all they could do was take off going 100 miles an hour away from it. Now, when I read the Bible 1st Corinthians the 15th chapter,

38.41st verse, But GOD giveth it a body as it has pleased him and every seed his own body.

39. All flesh is not the same flesh: but there is one kind of flesh of men, another flesh of beast, another of fishes, and another of birds.

40. There are also celestial bodies, and bodies terrestrial: but the glory of the Celestial is one, and the glory of the terrestrial is another.

41. There is one glory of the sun, and another glory of the moon, and another glory of the stars, but one, star differeth from another star in glory.

Now I type this scripture because I was always taught that Celestial bodies were angels, and terrestrial bodies were, well you know. LOL, why did it say all flesh. So, is area 51 real, Things that make you say hmmmmmmmm.

Women's Clothing

This is one scripture that men are always throwing in women's faces. Like they don't remember that back in the day before pants were invented men wore dresses. I'm talking about Deuteromony 22:5 The woman shall not wear that which pertaineth to a man. Neither shall a man put on a woman's garment: for all that do so are abomination unto the Lord thy God. I had to ask God about that scripture over, and over again and this is what I got from the spirit. God made Adam and Eve not, well you know the rest lol. And I don't have anything against gay people, but when you read Ezekiel 3:17-21, or 1st Corinthians 6: 9 & 10.

You will understand why a warning always comes before destruction. I'm giving you this as a warning, please take heed. Also please note that it's in all capital letters or red ink, which means GOD is speaking.

Ezekiel 3:17 – 21

17.SON OF MAN, I HAVE MADE THEE A WATCHMAN UNTO THE HOUSE OF ISREAL: THERE FORE HEAR THE WORD AT MY MOUTH, AND GIVE THEM WARNING FROM ME.

18. WHEN I SAY UNTO THE WICKED THOU SHALT SURELY DIE: AND THOU GIVETH HIM NOT WARNING, NOR SPEAKEST TO WARN THE WICKED FROM HIS WICKED WAYS, TO SAVE HIS LIFE; THE SAME WICKED MAN SHALL DIE IN HIS INIQUITY: BUT HIS BLOOD WILL I REQUIRE AT THINE HAND.

19. YET IF THOU WARN THE WICKED, AND HE TURN NOT FROM HIS WICKEDNESS, NOR FROM HIS WICKED WAYS, HE SHALL DIE IN HIS INIQUITY: BUT THOU HAST DELIVERED THY SOUL.

20. AGAIN, WHEN A RIGHTEOUS MAN DOTH TURN FROM HIS RIGHTEOUSNESS, AND COMMIT INIQUITY, AND I LAY A STUMBLINGBLOCK BEFORE HIM, HE SHALL DIE: BECAUSE THOU HAST NOT GIVEN HIM WARNING, HE SHALL DIE IN HIS SIN, AND HIS RIGHTEOUSNESS WHICH HE HATH DONE SHALL NOT BE REMEMBERED; BUT HIS BLOOD WILL I REQUIRE AT THINE HAND.

21. NEVERTHELESS IF THOU WARN THE RIGHTEOUS MAN, THAT THE RIGHTEOUS SIN NOT, AND HE DOTH NOT SIN, HE SHALL SURELY LIVE, BECAUSE HE IS WARNED: ALSO THOU HATH DELIVERED THY SOUL.

GOD is saying here, if you know that someone is committing a sin, or keeps doing the same sin over and over, and you don't say anything to warn them, their blood is on your hands. Just tell them one time, where it would touch their spirit, and bother them to where they can't sleep unless they change their ways, then their blood in not on your hands. Because you made and effort to help them. A warning always comes before destruction.

1st Corinthians 6: 9 & 10

9.Know yea not that the unrighteous shall not inherit the kingdom of God? Be not deceived: neither fornicators, nor idolaters, nor adulterers, nor effeminate, nor abusers of themselves with mankind,

10.Nor thieves, nor covetous, nor drunkards, shall inherit the Kingdom of God.

If you don't know the meaning to those words, look them up in the dictionary. The one I want you to look up is effeminate. You still have time to repent and turn your life around. Here is another scripture you may want to see. Everyone wants to know if its wrong to get tattoos. I don't think GOD holds it against you if you got them and didn't know. But I would ask for forgiveness and repent, and never get anymore. The book of Leviticus has a lot of rules and laws, you may want to read it. 15th chapter tells how a woman should not sleep with a man when she is on her menstrual period. Chapter 17 tells how eating flesh with blood is forbidden. Chapter 18 talks about sexual morality, who not to have sex with. And chapter 19 is instructions for holy living. Verse 28 is about tattoos. It says, capital letters, YE SHALL NOT MAKE ANY CUTTINGS IN YOUR FLESH FOR THE DEAD, NOR PRINT ANY MARKS UPON YOU: I AM THE LORD. All of what I just said is not to hurt you, GOD allows us to repent for our sins. No one in this world today is perfect. Everybody sins. 1st John, not the book of John, but this book is located two books before the book of Revelations. 1st John 1: verses 8 – 10.

8. If we say that we have no sin, we deceive ourselves, and the truth is not in us.

9. If we confess our sins, HE is faithful and just to forgive us our sins, and to cleanse us from all unrighteousness.

10. If we say that we have not sinned, we make HIM a liar, and HIS word is not in us.

The 2nd verse is as important. It talks about the light of GOD in us and keeping HIS commandments. One of the commandments that a lot of people have a problem with is honoring their mother and father. The bible tells us to do that, and that our days would be longer, but have you seen some of these parents out there. Parents you need to know this stuff.

Santa

I'm not saying to you if he's real or not, people made him what he is today. Fat, jolly, have reindeers, have magic, goes up and down chimneys, gave him elves. But if you read Zechariah 2:6, all capital letters;

6. HO, HO, COME FORTH, AND FLEE FROM THE LAND OF THE NORTH, saith the LORD: FOR I HAVE SPREAD YOU ABROAD AS THE FOUR WINDS OF THE HEAVENS, saith the LORD.

Now, I don't care how you choose to interpret this. Just remember man made him what he is today.

Witchcraft

2nd Chronicles 33:6   And he caused his children to pass through the fire in the Valley of the son of Hinnorn: also he observed times, and used enchantments, and used witchcraft and dealt with a familiar spirit, and with Wizards: He wrought much evil in the sight of the LORD to provoke him to anger.

1st Samuel 15:23 For rebellion is a sin of witchcraft, and stubbornness is as iniquity and idolatry. Because thou hast rejected the word of the LORD, he hath also rejected thee from being king.

Leviticus 19:31 REGARD NOT THEM THAT HAVE A FAMILIAR SPIRIT, NEITHER SEEK AFTER WIZARDS, TO BE DEFILED BY THEM: I AM THE LORD YOUR GOD.

Satyrs

OK, you all know what these are, half man, half beast. But, yet, the bible speaks of them in two scriptures, both in the book of Isaiah.

Isaiah 13:21 – (capital letters again which means GOD is talking.) BUT WILD BEASTS OF THE DESERT SHALL LIE THERE; AND THEIR HOUSES SHALL BE FULL OF DOLEFUL CREATURES; AND OWLS SHALL DWELL THERE, AND SATYRS SHALL DANCE THERE.

Isaiah 34:14 The wild beasts of the desert shall also meet with the wild beasts of the island, and the satyr shall cry to his fellow; the screech owl also shall rest there; and find for herself a place to rest.

Dragons

Isaiah 13:22 (caps) AND THE WILD BEAST OF THE ISLANDS SHALL CRY IN THE DESOLATE HOUSES, AND DRAGONS IN THEIR PLEASANT PALACES: AND HER TIME IN THE NEAR TO COME, AND HER DAYS SHALL NOT BE PROLONGED.

Now the book of Revelations talks a lot about dragons. But that's a book I think everyone should read from the beginning to the end. So, if you want to know more about them, read the book of Revelations. That book is hard for a lot of people to read because they think it's scary. But it lets you know what's gonna happen to you when JESUS comes back, and other things you really need to hear.

Adding Words, or Taking Words from the Bible

Revelation 22:18 & 19

18.For I testify until every man that hear the words of the prophecy of this book, if any man shall add unto these things, GOD shall add unto him the plagues that are written in this book.

19.And if any man should take away from the words of the book of this prophecy, GOD shall take away his part out of the book of life, and out of the holy city, and from the things which are written in this book.

The reason why I added that scripture is because now days you hear people saying they need these new international versions of the bible to understand a lot of what's in the bible. Why don't you just ask GOD to give you the wisdom and knowledge to understand what you read in the bible. I say that because a lot of these new bibles has taken out the word CHRIST and LORD. Where it used to say CHRIST JESUS our LORD, it just says JESUS. Also, in the book of Genesis where it says, and darkness was upon the face of the deep, they changed the word upon to hovered over. Everyone knows if something is hovering over something, it's not touching it. But the word upon mean it's touching it. It was up on it. There are so many other places they thought changing the words would make you understand better, but how can you have a bible that takes the words CHRIST and LORD out of it.

 Well this is my first book. I hope you all enjoyed reading it as much as I enjoyed writing it. In closing I would just like to say...Parents, stop speaking negative and harsh things to your kids just because you are angry. Pronounce great things over them and watch them be somebody... Don't base things in your life on what people believe, base things on your life that you believe...Stop listening to negative people who never have anything good to say about anyone. Especially about you. People can't make you or break you unless you allow them to. Never give anyone that much power over you. Some people don't want you to exceed in anything. And never let them take away your dreams or visions. GOD made you, not man. Greater is HE that is in you, than he that is in the world. You can do all things, not some, all, thru CHRIST whom strengthens you. If you want to stop smoking, stop hanging around people who do. If you don't want to be a bully, stop hanging around them. Oh, and all of you with the potty mouths, James the 3rd chapter talks about that tongue.

Verse 9. Therewith bless we GOD, even the FATHER; and therewith curse we men, which are made after the similitude of GOD.

Verse 10. Out of the same mouth proceedeth blessings and cursing. My brethren, these things ought not to be.

Verse 11. Doth a fountain send forth at the same time sweet water and bitter?

Verse 12. Can the big tree, my brethren, bear olive berries? Even a vine, figs? So can no fountain both yield saltwater and fresh. I know it's hard for some of you to stop having a potty mouth, but at least try not to.

Have a blessed rest of your life. I dedicate this book to all my family, friends and enemies. For years and years and years to come!